From the Natural Man to the Spiritual Man

DR. KENNETH Z. FAIRBANKS

DEDICATION

I want to dedicate this book to God and Jesus Christ who gave me the wisdom, knowledge and vision to write this book.

In loving memory of my parents, the late Mr. Willie B. & Mrs. Maggie Fairbanks who gave me life, love, and raised me to be the man I am today.

My loving wife, Mrs. Nerita Higgins Fairbanks, for her prayers, support and encouragement in writing this book, and our children, Tammy, Tonya Kenneth Jr., Patrick, Robert and Jason.

My brothers and sisters, Walter, Ann, Robert, Freddie, Rose, Eddie and Gregory for their prayers and support.

.

CONTENTS

ACKNOWLEDGMENTS

I would like to thank the Father, Son and the Holy Spirit for guiding me in writing this book.

To my spiritual family at New Vision Ministries Church for their prayers, love and loyal support in the Ministry.

My brothers and sisters, Walter, Ann, Robert, Freddie, Rose, Eddie, and Gregory who love me and are a great resource for me.

My grandparents, the late Mr. Robert & Mrs. Rosie Mae Fairbanks.

Reverend Homer Davis and Pastor William Spears who assisted me in the transition from a natural man to a spiritual man.

New Testament Baptist Church where I joined as a member.

Dr. E.B. Tate. Ph. D of Rainbow Seminary School of Ministry in Alachua, Florida where I received my Doctor of Divinity Degree.

Our publisher, Mrs. Christine Wilson for her knowledge, expertise and dedication in making my dream come true.

John 15:7
If ye abide in me, and my words abide in you, ye shall ask what ye will, and it shall be done unto to you.

May each and every one who reads this book receive a blessing from God in Christ Jesus' name.

INTRODUCTION

From the Natural Man to the Spiritual Man describes my life story of growing up in Shellman, Georgia. I was born *Kenneth Zackery Fairbanks* on February 21, 1954. My father, Willie B. Fairbanks was a share cropper and my mother, Maggie Fairbanks, who always said that I was born with a vail over my face, was a homemaker. I was one out of eight children. Two are now deceased.

Very few people remember things that happened early in life, but I have total recall. At the age of two, I was cared for by my grandmother who was a hardworking woman who believed in the Lord. She purchased a bicycle for a Christmas gift that will forever be in my heart.

I was very different—often described as a loner and a very independent person. Throughout my life I experienced several setbacks and I didn't realize that it was a part of God's plan for my spiritual new birth.

I survived the streets of New York after running away from home at an early age. I lead a life of crime that included drugs and alcohol that caused my life to be threatened. Facing death, I realized that I couldn't survive on my own. The opposition that I faced was an opportunity to accept Jesus Christ as my Lord and Savior.

God had a plan for my life. Without God, I would not have the opportunity to tell this story. My testimony has and will continue to inspire readers and listeners to repent and seek the face of the Lord. As you read, just think about the goodness of Jesus and all that He had done for in your life.

2 Corinthians 5:17
Therefore, if any man be in Christ, he is a new creature; old things are passed away; behold all things are become new.

1

SURE FOUNDATION

At an early age, I danced at a place called James Green. I was taken there by my older sisters. One night when leaving the club, a big black snake came out of a bush at me. My sister ran the snake off as it continued to attack me. My family believed this was an indication that Satan was out to destroy my life.

My mother and father separated when I was young. My father liked to drink and have other relationships outside of his marriage. He worked very hard Monday through Friday and left home on the weekends. He had a very bad drinking problem. Where ever he laid his hat was his home.

I moved to Cocoa, Florida with my mother and her family. Five of my other brothers and sisters stayed with their grandparents. This was hurtful and I missed them very much. My mother worked at different hotels on the beach. One day I went to work with her because she did not have a babysitter.   Outside of the hotel a dog was heard barking and I went to investigate.   I started following the dog that went to the ocean bank.

Out of the dog's barking, I heard these words, "come closer, come closer." It was a sign of the enemy's attempt to destroy me.   A hotel worker and my mother started shouting for me to stand still and don't go any closer. The dog kept barking, and I heard again, "come closer, come closer". The hotel worker reached out and grabbed my foot. This prevented me from going over the bank.

I remember my father coming to Cocoa, Florida. He worked at the Kennedy Space Center for six months. We missed Georgia very much and decided to move back to be with my brothers, sisters and grandparents.

I was happy again at the age of five, gazing at the stars and the moonlight at night and dreaming of heaven.

My grandfather had hogs and chickens.   One day a hog got out of the pen, ran me down and trampled me. Trying to destroy me, the pig kept attacking me.   My grandfather beat the hog in head—almost killing him. My mind wondered, "Why is all this happening to me?"

My parents purchased their own house and my brothers and sisters moved out of my grandparents' house. Being school age, I was so happy. Taking peanut butter and jelly sandwiches was a blessing. Coming home in the afternoons from Shellman Vocational High, my sisters' friends would visit and eat food that my parents kept. I was playing basketball, enjoying baseball, and having sex with my sister's friend at the age of six.   I didn't know what to do, but my brothers showed me.

One day after school, I fell into an outside toilet and

had snakes swimming all around me. The toilet was twenty feet deep in raw sewage. I didn't know how to swim and was about to die. My friend heard me cry for help and my brothers and sisters called my mother who got a rope to help pull me out. Something was holding me and didn't want to let me go. Something supernaturally helped me to catch hold of the rope so I could get out. Even at six-years-old, I knew that I was different.

During the summer, school was out and my sister would have friends over to the house and they would offer sex to my brother for a piece of my mother's tobacco. I would see them having sex. I would say, "I'm going to tell if I don't get none." My brothers would put me on top of the girl and roll my behind around. After two minutes or so, I would get up and say, "Ahhh."

My parents took me to see a friend of theirs one night. They were standing around the bed—praying for her. I was standing and looking and saw baby snakes coming out of her mouth. Everyone praying had their eyes closed and I cried out, "snakes, snakes!"

They shouted, "kill them, kill them!" Everyone was throwing objects and stepping on them. All the snakes were killed and the lady rose from the bed. A voice said, "I wanted you to see that." I didn't know what it meant.

Between the age of seven and nine, I was picking cotton, hoeing peanuts and pulling corn. In the summertime in the cotton field of Shellman, Georgia, an incident happened. A big black snake came after me while I was sitting on a pile of cotton trying to keep cool. The snake was trying to bite me. I was still wondering why so many snakes were after me.

2

THE EARLY YEARS

My family moved from one house to another in the country. We were playing on a bale of hay and found six snakes when we moved the bale. One of the snakes bit my brother. I ran to the house and prayed, asking the Lord, "What is happening to me?" My brother was alright after my father took him to the doctor.

My father stopped farming and picked up a job in town. He worked as a maintenance technician in Shellman.

Three days later, a snake came into the house through a hole. Nobody could kill the snake and he got away. The next day no one was able to find the snake. Three days later, the same snake came back. I believe he was poisonous. He was in my room. I had to kill the snake. I heard a voice say, "This is going to be your job from now on."

After my father started working, we bought our own land and built a house. In our new home my life was changing. I was more mature. My father built a club on the back of our house. He had a pool table and sold moonshine. I started selling moonshine at the age of 10. I was selling more than my mother and father. My sister was my partner and we didn't give our parents all the money. We had the responsibility of keeping up with the money.

One night there was a shooting at the house and it seems like the bullet went right by my head. At ten years old, it really scared me. I knew that somebody was watching over me. I felt that I was supposed to die.

A friend of mine became upset with me for having sex with his girlfriend and he tried to cut me with a butcher's knife. My brother saved me by pushing him to the ground.

My parents opened another nightclub downtown. Learning how to dance, I loved to two-step. I could cook, and I sold hot dogs and hamburgers. People who were drinking loved to buy food. I would wear suits on Friday and Saturdays. I even wore them to school.

I started hanging with my brother who was four years older than I was. He taught me how to love and seek after women. I started taking moonshine and orange juice to school. I gave some to everybody in the school, including the seventh and eighth graders.

At least one hundred people left the schoolyard and went to a club during school hours. My sister went along too. We were caught by our school principal. Someone told on us. We got whippings and were suspended from school for two days. One day, when I went back to school, an older boy walked up to me and hit me in the stomach with his fist. I really thought I was going to die. If it had not been for my brother who stopped him, he was going to hit me over the head with a bottle.

At the age of 14, my brother and I went into business with one of our cousins. No one in Shellman knew anything about marijuana. My cousin planted a whole acre of marijuana in the projects. Oh yeah, he was the same cousin who skinned a cow and a hog in the bath tub. We stole the animals. When the marijuana harvest was ready, my cousin gave me and my brother a fifty-gallon size garbage bag full of it. He told us to sale what we could and to do what we wanted to because it all belonged to us.

We taught everyone, young and old, men and women, in the club how to smoke the marijuana. We started making money. After we sold a single bag, and at the age of 15, I was able to get my learner's driving license. My father would not sign for us to get a car. One of our neighbors took us to get the car and signed for us. We paid two thousand dollars for a 1967 Ford Galaxy, three on the collar.

My brother didn't know how to drive the car. I would drive my brother around to sell the marijuana. I even drove him into the corn field to have sex with women. That same night, we were run out of Dawson, Georgia. People were shooting at us and bullets hit the car. They didn't like me. Thank God we made it back home to Shellman, Georgia. They were mad because we were taking their girls.

We took a bag of marijuana back to Dawson, Georgia. I met the most beautiful girl that I had ever seen at that time. I thought about trying to be nice and right for her. My own brother, another guy, and I starting fighting over this girl. I ran to the car and got my shot gun. The enemy said to me, "shoot them all." I didn't. I just shot into the air and we got back in the car and went back to Shellman, Georgia.

3

RUNNING AWAY FROM HOME

Coming up to the age of 16, my brother left me and went into the military. That same year, my father bought a new car. I wanted to go pick up my girlfriend before it was too late in the evening. He said, "No! Get in that kitchen." I would cook hamburgers and hot dogs for the club in the back of the house. My daddy left the house for the club across town where my mother was. I heard a voice say to get fifty dollars out of the cash register and leave—just go.

Around 1 a.m. the following morning, I locked the doors. My mother and father were not at home. A friend came by the house and I caught a ride with him to Dawson, Georgia. He dropped me off at the bus station. I told him that I was going to New York. I asked the ticket agent the cost of a one-way ticket. He told me it was $48.00, and that the ride would be take 48 hours. I only had $50.00 in my pocket. After buying the ticket, I had

$2.00 left. By the time we got to Atlanta, Georgia I was hungry. I should have eaten and taken more clothes before I left home. In Virginia, I ate a candy bar. By Baltimore, I was so hungry my mouth was white. I knew it was the supernatural because a man got on the bus in Baltimore and his mother had cooked him a whole chicken.

He looked at me, realizing that I was hungry, and asked me if I wanted a piece of chicken. He gave me a chicken breast. I ate it so fast; I believe I ate the bones too! He said, "Boy you are hungry! Take another piece." For the first time I mentioned God. I said, "Thank you, God."

When we arrived in Washington, D.C., the same man who gave me the chicken got drunk on the bus and the bus driver left him. There was no more food. We arrived in New York at night. We traveled across the George Washington Bridge and, seeing all the bright lights, I didn't know what the next move was going to be.

Getting off the bus at the port authority, I had fifty cents left. I went to a bench and stayed there until the next morning. I was lonely and hungry and had nobody to talk to. I was on my own and my mother, father, brother and sisters were not there.

I walked three and four miles a day and ate scraps from trash cans at different restaurants. The only place I knew to go was back to the bus station. Seeing how beautiful New York City was after four days, I used one of my quarters to call one of my sisters. When I called, nobody answered the telephone, so I waited until the next day and I tried to call back.

My brother-in-law answered the phone and asked me

where I was. I told him that I was at the bus station. He told me to wait and he would pick me up and that he would be driving a gypsy cab. About two hours later, he picked me up and took me to Bronx where my sister and their two children lived. When I saw her, I cried and hugged her.

She said she had talked to our mother and father. My mother wanted me to come back home, but my father would not send for me. I told my sister, "When I get back to Georgia, I'll be a man." After a week with my sister and her family, her friend's husband had left some military clothes with her. Her friend said that I could have the clothes if I would have sex with her. So I stayed all night.

Back at my sister's house, I said "We could make some money." I was handsome and fine. Ladies were coming after me. As a matter of fact, a twenty-one-year old girl, weighing about 300 pounds, kicked in a door at my sister's house. She took advantage and raped me. I cried that night. When my sister came home, I told her what happened. They were mad because the door was off the hinges. I told them to call the police, but they would not.

As time went on, I went out and I met my brother-in-law's brother. He was a pimp in New York and taught me the pimping game in order to gain control of women's minds. He taught me that any man can control a woman's body, but, if you want her, you must learn how to control her mind.

So, I was in the street hustling, making money, and living a fast life. I went back to my sister's house. One night we were at a club that was located on the first floor of the apartments at 179th and Washington Ave. I partied all night long and came out of the club at 9 a.m. the next morning. I ate breakfast with friends who were in a group called the Persuaders. They had a hit record— "It's a Thin Line between Love and Hate."

Being new on the scene, as they practiced at the same club I would go to, they asked me to be their protégé. I helped set up their equipment on the dance floor and arranged their clothes. It was a party scene that I had never seen.

I was getting high every day. One night, I didn't go out of town with the group. I stayed in the club and partied until 3 a.m. and got into an argument with some gang bangers at the club over some girls. I got mad and went upstairs and got a sawed-off shot gun. I shot up the club. I thank God, I didn't hit anyone. My friend took me back upstairs so I could sleep. Someone had called the police, but the police could not find me. I woke up at about six that morning. I walked into another bedroom asking for my sister. There was another woman that I had never seen. I asked who she was. She was my brother-in-law's sister. I said, "It's not anyone here but me and you."

I crawled into the bed and she hollered out, "What are you doing?" I told her I was Skin, Ann's brother. The lady said my sister had told her about me. She asked me repeatedly to get out of the bed. I didn't get out of the bed and I started playing with her. She told me to stop and that she had a six-year-old and that she had not had sex. She was a Jehovah's Witness. I didn't stop, and we had sex.

I couldn't remember much about that day, but four months later, my sister came in and woke me up. She said that I had been bad and that some people had come to see me. I got up and went into the kitchen. There was the mother of the woman I'd been with and four other people from the Kingdom Hall who questioned me about having sex. I told them that I didn't really know, but the sitter said we did. Her mother said that I would have to marry her or else. She couldn't remain a Jehovah's Witness otherwise. I told her mother that I wasn't going to marry anyone.

So, she was no longer a Jehovah's Witness and was put out of the apartment because of me. A couple of months later, one my friends and I came home. My brother-in-law had my sister tied up. We pulled out our knives and my brother-in-law pulled out his shot gun. He told us to get out of his house. I told him that I would cut him. My friend kept telling me, "Skin, come on let's go." I told my friend that my sister does all the work and my brother-in-law doesn't work. My brother-in-law pleaded with my sister for me to leave.

One of my sister's friends who lived across the hall saw what was going on. She asked my friend and I to leave because my brother-in-law had a shot gun. She told him that he shouldn't do his wife that way. He said, "This is my house and my wife and I will do what I want to do." My sister asked me to please leave. I left with nowhere to stay. I only had the clothes on my back. My friend had a kitchenette and told me I could stay with him until I found a place.

I slept on the floor for three months. I was hustling and doing what I could do to survive on the streets of New York. One day I was riding by 179th street where my sister lived. I saw my brother-in-law outside with my sister. I ran up to him and body slammed him. I started beating him and his sister said to me, "Don't kill him. I'm pregnant, Skin. Don't kill him." When I let him go, he ran.

His sister said to me, "I'm pregnant and I need to talk

to you." They had been looking for me for about three months and couldn't find me. My sister told me that she was sorry that I had to leave that night. She didn't want me to get hurt.

My brother-in-law's sister told me that she had an apartment. She gave me a key to visit her anytime. The next day I went to visit her. She talked to me about going to school to get an education. I could work in the day and go to school at night. I moved in with her a month later. She helped me to get a work permit.

My friend that I had stayed with the previous three months helped me to get a job. Going to school and working was hard. She kept getting bigger. I was partying, drinking, and leaving her alone. I was also messing with other women.

I met another friend who was a longshoreman. He asked if I wanted to make some big money. I told him "yes." He brought me one hundred pistols and I sold them for one hundred dollars a piece. He would buy them cheap overseas for ten and fifteen dollars in American money. We were making money. I made thirty thousand and gave him the rest of seventy thousand. I was in the game doing well.

I moved my pregnant girlfriend to a better neighborhood. I furnished everything. I stopped working my job and started working the streets. I could feel that somebody was watching over me.

My baby sister and her friend came from Georgia to Newark. They hadn't got married yet. Shortly thereafter, they got married. I gave her away in the wedding. It was a joyous occasion.

A month later, I called my brother in law and told him that I needed to talk to him. I was seventeen. I caught a train down town to Manhattan. I was heading to Newark when I met a man and his wife. I was high on cocaine and we began talking. He told me that his wife was going to upstate New York to visit her parents. I told him that I was going to visit my relatives. He told me that he worked in Newark and I could ride with him. I got into the car with him. He needed to change clothes so we went to his home. It was a nice mansion. He pulled into the garage and invited me into his house.

The first thing he handed me was a book about a nude man. He went to take a shower. Something wasn't right. I wondered why he showed me the book. He came out of the shower and asked me to lay down with him. I asked him if he was crazy. I told him that I didn't do that. He grabbed my hand and said that no one would know. I broke away from him, picked up a lamp, and started breaking things in the house. He told me to stop and not to tear up his wife's house.

I asked for his car keys and threatened to break up other items in the house. He asked me not to call the police and gave me the keys. I told him that he could find his car in Newark. I threatened to harm him if he came around me. I left in the car and parked the car five blocks from my sister's house. I left the key inside the car.

I told my sister what had happened. She said that he was probably gay and on the down low. I had never experienced anything like that before.

My bother-in-law told me that I could probably get a job with him working on the dock. I was so pleased. I stayed with him and my sister that weekend. I put an application in that Monday. He worked as a crane operator. I was hired the same day.

I was a dock safety worker and made $22 an hour. I awoke at 4 a.m. and went to Newark. I bought my first car and tried working and staying out of the streets.

4

LIFE IN THE CITY

I kept selling guns. I used drugs and was involved with a lot of women. I stayed with my baby's mother. Living the life, I had saved sixty thousand dollars. Come to find out my girlfriend was pregnant again. I tried to make it.

My best friend received a check because of an injury for one hundred and twenty-five thousand dollars. We flew to Shellman, Georgia. It was the first time I had seen my mom and dad since leaving home. Turning age 18, I prayed and asked my parents to forgive me. My mother cried and told me I broke her heart.

In Georgia, I gave my dad five thousand dollars. I was drinking gallons of moonshine. People had never seen that before. We weren't afraid of the police or anybody. After partying for a week, we went back to New

York. I was still working. I got involved again with my girlfriend's brother who worked for the Mafia. He needed my help. He had a contract to kill his sister's husband. I talked to him because I knew them both. He asked me what to do since he had the contract. He risked getting himself killed. For the second time in my life, I said, "Let's pray."

Later that night I went back to my girlfriend's house. I received a call that my best friend had shot his brother-in-law who owed the Mafia some money. He shot him twice, but he didn't die.

The streets are a dangerous place. I also got caught up in the game. Three weeks later we found my girlfriend's brother dead. Somebody killed him because he didn't finish the contract. I was all broken up and took a trip to Baltimore. Coming home at three o'clock in the morning, I was high on cocaine. I told my girlfriend to get up and make me something to eat. She wouldn't do it. Being angry, I drugged her out of the bed. She ran into the bathroom and locked the door. I took my thirty-two automatic and shot twice into the bathroom. She hollered that I shot her.

I left $100,000 worth of clothes and twenty-five pistols. My check book was under the mattress. I left and went to uptown Bronx and stayed with one of my friends. I was still partying and drinking. My girlfriend called the police that night.

I quit my job two weeks later. I was trying to figure out how to get back into the apartment without the police looking for me. I disguised myself by wearing a beard. My friend wanted to break into the apartment and I told him not to do it. As we watched the apartment early one morning, my girlfriend and our two daughters left. I was able to get into the apartment. The locks had not been changed. My check book was still under the mattress. I picked up as much of the jewelry as I could. The guns were gone. I didn't have enough time to get my clothes.

My friend and I went to the bank. He left, thinking that I might get caught by the police. I made it to the bank teller and told her that I wanted to withdraw $50,000.00. She looked at me and said that she would be right back. I said to myself, "I know they will catch me." By that time, the manager said, "Mr. Fairbanks will you come with me to my office?" I saw a police officer following us. The manager said, "This is your money, but the amount of the withdrawal needs an approval. I told him I understood. He asked me how I wanted the cash. I said, "In large bills, except for $500.00." The manager asked me if I had bought a house. I told him that I was going out of town. I asked him how much was in the account and he told me I had $60,000.00. I made a withdrawal of $30,000.00 and left $30,000.00 in my girlfriend's name. I confirmed the request and left the bank with the cash.

My friend could not believe that I had gotten away with it. I opened my briefcase and showed him the cash. He asked me, "Skin, where are you going?" I told him I was going to Jacksonville, Florida and then I caught a cab.

I asked the driver how much the fare was to the port authority and the Kennedy airport. When I got into the cab, I told him to take me to the Newark airport. The cost was $100.00. Going into the airport, I watched my surroundings while I purchased my ticket.

The plane was leaving for Jacksonville, Florida in ten minutes. I got on the plane and had a layover in Atlanta for one hour. I was holding two briefcases, one with gold and the other with money. People were watching me. One man asked if I was a salesman. I asked him if I looked like one. He said that he noticed the briefcases. After that, I went to the bathroom and a man tried to steal one of the briefcases. After we wrestled, I finally got the advantage. Someone came into the bathroom. I told him I was going to call the police.

Leaving the bathroom, the announcement was made to board the plane to Jacksonville. When I arrived, I called my oldest brother to pick me up. I met up with another brother who just come from Germany. We had a good time together. I showed them the jewelry, but not the money. My older brother was glad we were in town and said we could find a job.

Three weeks later, he was moving and said my brother and I could keep the apartment. We agreed to take the apartment. Neither one of us was working at the time. I showed my brother who had come from Germany the $30,000.00. He had $20,000.00. Let the party begin!

We partied day and night. The guys would meet up, and called our apartment the bachelor pad. The drugs and the women continued. I was the corporal and everyone wanted to be like me. I went and bought $2,000.00 worth of clothes.

One day I looked off the balcony and there was a girl going to school. When she came from school, I asked her name and how old she was. I invited her up to the apartment. I was nineteen-years-old at the time. She was scared. I walked downstairs—all sharp and clean. Her mother came outside and I introduced myself. I had lived there for a few months. She said her son had told her I was from New York. I said, "Yes ma'am. That's me."

She asked if I was looking at her daughter—saying she was only sixteen. I was invited to their house. She said that she often heard the music and girls. She stated that my brother and I didn't work.

She asked me if I wanted a beer. After I found out she drank beer, I bought a case. We sat that evening and talked and drank until midnight. The father in the bedroom. When the mother went to sleep on the couch, I took their daughter upstairs to my apartment.

She was a virgin and wanted to have sex. We had sex for the first time and I took her home around 1 a.m. I went back upstairs and called my friends over to party.

I had not worked in over a year. The next day, my cousin came over. We talked and he told me that he had a job for me. He had some Italian friends who liked to watch people have sex. I went with him. There were two women in his bed and two in another bed. Three men were watching behind a mirror. We were paid five hundred dollars apiece. It was some easy money, and we enjoyed doing something we liked. He offered to call me in another week if I liked it.

A week later my friend brought one of the Italian men to our bachelor pad. He wanted to talk to me about moving a car from Orlando to Jacksonville, Florida. He offered to give me $500.00. I did that, not knowing that the car probably was full of drugs. We became friends and he started bringing me all types of drugs to get rid of for him. I started selling drugs and made $5,000.00 a week.

Everyone knew me as Skin. My brother told me not to get involved too deep because that was the Mafia. I took his warning and quit after six months. My brother and I went to look for a job. We wanted to wait awhile because we still had money.

5

THE TRANSITION

The young girl told me after eight weeks that she was pregnant. She was still in high school. I told her not to worry and that I would take care of the baby. Still partying and not working, another friend of ours came to us. He said that he worked for the Trail Way bus station. He told me he had gotten twenty pounds of marijuana off the bus. It was Columbia gold. He gave me and my brother ten pounds. We smoked and sold it and partied. About six months later the friend who gave us the marijuana got jacked. He said it was the Mafia who said the marijuana belonged to them.

My brother and I heard about the raid. We went to my friend's apartment and starting shooting it out with the Mafia in the apartment. They left and said they would be back. Nobody got hurt. I told my brother I wanted to find a job. The following week we went to the Jacksonville shipyard. We were hired on the spot. We really didn't want the job, but we took it anyway. We had money and were making money.

I was still partying and meeting people on the ship who brought drugs into the US. I would buy drugs and flip it, and also worked on the shipyard. I was living the life of a gangster. When I walked into a club, everyone knew who I was.

One summer the shipyard paid us to go to Miami on a work detail—all expenses paid. I partied for three months in Miami City. I told my brother something wasn't right. The company paid for our coworkers to rent a car, but did not pay for ours.

Back in Jacksonville, we filed a complaint against the white workers. They told us we would get fired if went to the labor broad, so we quit. We were still selling marijuana that eventually ran out. The money started to get low. I started strip dancing at parties.

Leaving work at 3 a.m. one morning, I was high on drugs. I drove my car off the Main Street Bridge in Jacksonville, Fl. The bridge was 50 feet high. The car went one way and I went the other way. Before the police found me, I had swum to the bank. I saw an angel watching over me. I was taken to the hospital, and then to jail. The next morning, I was released because of the laws in Florida. I could get out of jail with a signature bond.

My son was born and I was still selling drugs. Six months later I broke up with his mother. She started dating other people and so did I. One morning I found all four of my tires slashed on my car. I confronted her mother and brothers. They got mad and wanted to jump me and I threatened to shoot them. My son's family was upset with me and said something was going to happen to me.

At the age of 21, I was still making a little money. My friend asked me if I had a pound of marijuana. He could get six hundred dollars for it. I was riding in a 2802 let back convertible when we went out to sell the marijuana. We stopped to get some gas and were surrounded by drug agents. I was told to get out of the car. The police said. "Alias, Skin, we finally got you." They looked under the car seat and found the marijuana. I told them that it wasn't mine. They told me that I would get locked up and took me to jail. I was arrested for possession of one pound of marijuana. They did not take the driver.

I had to call my oldest brother to come and get me out of jail. I told him that somebody set me up. He took me back to the apartment. Another lady that I was seeing came to visit and my baby's mother and her mother beat her up. I heard the noise. She was on the ground. She came by to tell me that she was pregnant. I called the ambulance because she was beaten badly.

I rode with her to the hospital and told her to report the incident to the police. We left the hospital around 3 a.m. that morning. Everything started to go wrong. I made it back to the apartment. I went downstairs and kicked the door in at my baby's mother house. I started fighting her family members. I was high on drugs and ran them out of the apartment.

The police never came. I was like a wild man and my brother came and got me. They said that I would never see my son again.

6

BACK TO GEORGIA

I started to work for the city of Jacksonville as a pipefitter. I was still making money, dating, drinking and partying. I began to feel down on myself. Something was still missing in my life. I know it was God because I got up one Sunday morning and went to a church. I started crying—tears running out of my eyes—and people started to look. I left service before it was over.

I snorted some cocaine and a friend came by the house. We took a ride to the beach. We picked up a young lady who was eighteen-years-old. I brought her back to my apartment and she got high. There were 4 or 5 friends there and they pulled a train on her. They kept saying, "Skin, you go first." I refused. I was troubled and didn't have sex with her. I said, "Let's take her back to the beach." They repeatedly said that it wasn't like me. I asked why. It was because I had a conscience.

My friend was waiting on me after we got back from the beach. I had to go to court. I told him that he was going with me. I told him I thought I was set up. He said he wasn't going to court because they would lock him up. My other friends told him that if he didn't go to court, they didn't want to see him on the streets anymore.

I went to court and was charged with possession of one pound of marijuana and pleaded not guilty. A trial was set up and the judge asked if I needed a lawyer. I told him I would represent myself. The district attorney said the drugs were closer to me. I was asked if I had any witnesses. I had one who owned the car. I told the judge that I would prove to him that I was set up. I called a witness who testified we were just riding and the drug agent came in behind us. Because the drugs were closer to me, I was taken to jail. He went on to say that my name, "Skin," was called like I was being set up. He told the judge the car belonged to him. The judge asked why he wasn't locked up, and he said that he didn't know.

The two arresting officers were called as witnesses. The judge asked why both were not locked up and they told the judge that I was the only one they wanted. The judge told me I was free to go. I was released because everyone wasn't locked up. I didn't know what I was doing, but I said, "Thank you, Lord."

Leaving there, I was feeling good. I went back to the apartment and got high. I saw my son outside. His mother let me play with him for a few minutes. She wanted to talk to me. I had not made it upstairs to my apartment. I invited her up and we started talking. I made it to the door of my bedroom. When I opened the door, there was another woman in my bed.

I told her I didn't know who she was and she started

crying and ran back downstairs to her mother. I asked the lady who she was and how she got in my room. She replied that it was her brother. I made her get up and leave. I was kind of brokenhearted. My baby's mother thought she had another chance with me, but since the woman was in my bed, she told me to not ever speak to her again. She told me that I would never see my son.

I went into seclusion—not wanting to work. I knew it was time for a change. My brothers suggested that I go back to Georgia. I said, "That's what I'll do." So, I left Jacksonville, and left everything behind. When returning back to Georgia, I saw my mother, father and baby brothers.

I had no money in my pocket. I wasn't able to see my two baby girls in New York. I knew that God didn't want me to live like that anymore. I was enjoying my mother and daddy. My daddy told me he would give me his old truck if I took my mother to church. I thanked my dad and to told him that was fine. I wanted to do something good for them.

Several weeks later, I found a job working at a plywood company in Cuthbert, Georgia. I was making pretty good money. It was my first three hundred dollar pay check in a while. I had a friend take me back to Jacksonville to get a pound of marijuana. I sold the pound in one week at my job. I gained one thousand dollars from my three-hundred-dollar investment. I was back in the game again. I had drugs shipped to me in Georgia.

I started making three thousand dollars a week. Six months later, I bought a Lincoln Continental. I decided to open up a bar and a small night club. The county was dry and no alcohol could be sold. I bought alcohol in another county to supply my club. I made thousands of dollars and bought a new Cadillac. People wanted the drugs and alcohol, but didn't have access to it.

At age 22, I had an accident on the job. I was offered twenty thousand dollars. I resigned and opened up a bigger night club with a pool room and night club. I had over one hundred and twenty thousand dollars in my pocket. I was living the life. I was a small town pimp with prostitutes and plenty of money. I didn't know what to do with it.

Everybody loved me—including a few young people. Since I ran away from home at age 15, some young people didn't know me.

I asked my daddy to build a safe made of steel. We put over one hundred and twenty-five thousand dollars in the safe inside our house. I was enjoying my mom and daddy, and gave my mom whatever she wanted. It was so great to be home and be on top. In my heart, something was still missing.

I had an auntie and a cousin who came by one Saturday morning. They asked me to take a ride. I thought we were going to get something to eat. Instead, they took me to a place that I'd heard about but didn't think it was real. There was a root worker at this place. I asked them why I was brought there. They told me I was on top. And that's where I wanted to stay.

I went inside and the root worker asked me what I wanted. The root worker said, "You have the blessing of God on your life and you're coming to me?" My aunt and cousin told me to ask for some luck. I told the root worker I had opened up a night club that held over one thousand people. She gave me a bag to take and told me to sprinkle what was inside the bag on the floor. She said to sweep it up and put it back in the bag and take the bag across the street and drop it.

They told me to give the root worker some money. I said, "I don't believe in this stuff, I believe in God." I gave her fifty dollars anyway. Back in Shellman, my auntie and cousin put me out and said, "Try it."

I went up to the club and did what the root worker said. I threw the trash on the other side of the road. This was on a Friday night. That night there were fifteen hundred people at the club. It was packed. Can you imagine having that many people come into the club? The club was called the 747 Club. I had the alcohol, lights, women and drugs. I was making cash money.

People were jealous. One of the councilmen came to me and said he knew what I was doing. He said that if I wanted to keep the club open I would have to pay him. The mayor knew also what was going on. He didn't take any money because I was making money for the town. The town was making money like never before.

Something was still missing. My cousin introduced me to one of his cousins who was a school teacher. I thought marriage was missing, or at least a companion. I was riding around and everyone wanted me. This was a woman who was ten years older and was into church. I said to myself, "This might work." At the age of 23, I asked her to marry me. It wasn't for love; it was just somewhere to hide my money.

When the world offers you everything, there comes a time when you want somewhere to hide. Her family didn't like me because I was hustling to make money. I owned a club, a restaurant, and a pool hall. I bought five acres of land in Cuthbert, Georgia and bought her a trailer and a couple of cars. She had one daughter. Even as my wife, she didn't know anything about me. I started letting her into my circle. I let everybody at the club know that she was my wife.

The first night that happened, she got mad. She ran outside the club and sat in the car because ladies were kissing on me. She stayed in the car for three hours. I took her home and we argued and fussed the whole way. I went back to the club, which stayed open until 3 a.m.

Some people asked why I married her. It was because she was a school teacher and was very respectable. We were not compatible. I stayed in the marriage and tried to make it work. My wife would lock herself in the room and cry. On Sunday mornings, she tried to get me to go to church and I wouldn't go.

The seeds you sow--you're going to reap them.

My cousins came to me and said I needed to go back to see the woman—the root worker. I told them I didn't need that woman—she was just a big liar. I didn't believe in it. She said that if I didn't come back I would lose everything.

The sheriff came by that Saturday night to find drugs and alcohol so a case could be brought against me. I had already paid the commissioner who told me a raid was coming through that night, so I hid everything, including the drugs, alcohol, and money. I had a place to bury it. They searched and could not find a trace of anything.

He started asking me questions. He knew my daddy and wanted to know where all these people had come from. That night, I had over one thousand people in the club. The sheriff said that I would not make money like I

41

had been unless he was a part of it. He called me a liar when I told him that I hadn't made any money. He told me that he had been watching and if he could not be a part that he would shut me down.

There were three neighbors in the neighborhood who wanted thirty dollars a week for me to stay open. As I struggled to keep the club open, my cousins and aunt wanted me to go back to the root worker. I told them again that I wasn't going back down there because I didn't believe in it.
.

After saying that, I was riding to Cuthbert and hit a deer. I tore up my Lincoln Continental. While it was being fixed, I went and paid cash for a cream Deuce and a Quarter. I saw people following me in the country. It was four or five white people in a truck that tried to run me off the road. They were yelling out the 'n' word and asking where the money was. It was just a blessing because, where they had me hemmed, no one would have known that I was there.

I started shooting with my pistol, saying "Lord, help me out of this." I could not see all of their faces because some of them had on masks. I didn't know if I hit anyone, but I made it out. I took the low road to Cuthbert.

I decided to pray that night because so much evil and pain was coming against me, and I didn't know what it was. I needed to go to my dad's house to get the money. When you dream about something and God gives you a vision, you need to do it.

At about noon the next day, I got a call from my mother's neighbor. She told me that I better get there because the house was on fire. By the time I got there, I saw all the flames. I first looked for my mother. My father was alright and so was my grandmother because her house was next door. It was a five-bedroom house, and all of our material things were destroyed—including the pictures. The house was a total loss.

My mom was crying and I told them not to worry about anything because I would take care of them. After every one left, I found myself sorting though the ruble. I was trying to find the box with the money in it that my dad had made for me. When we had finally found it, we opened it up. The money was crumbled up. The heat from the fire had destroyed it.

My mom was able to stay with my grandmother until they got a new trailer house. My brothers were going to help get the trailer. The following week, I got word from the city commissioner that they weren't going to shut my club down. The hours would change from closing at 3 a.m. to 10 p.m.

I tried that for about a month. Most people would just be coming out at 10. I closed the club and the pool house down.

7

FACING OPPOSITION

My cousin said that I should have gone back to the root worker. What do you do when people criticize you? You're on top one day, and then when you're down, no one tries to help you.

I know that the God I serve is able. After losing everything, except two cars, I found a job. I was working for this man out across a field—picking up sticks, cleaning off land, and driving a tractor. That was something I had never done before.

Still praying when I would get to the field in the morning, one of my coworker's hollered out and told me that God doesn't hear a sinner's prayer. And the other men said to be quiet let me pray. They said that I didn't have any business in the field working with them.

Leaving work, I had to go home to my wife in Cuthbert. My body was tired. It seemed like I was catching more hell from her, so I started putting on clothes and going to clubs around me. I was drinking and coming home late at night. I knew this wouldn't last.

My wife's father asked me to join this organization since I wasn't running the club. So I did and I was accepted. It was a blessing in disguise. We met every first and third Friday. Just about everyone in the group was not for real. We would leave the hall and go to the club.

One night at the club I met a lady who was beautiful. She asked me if I was the one who had owned the club. She said that she had visited the club several times. That same night, she asked me to take her home and I did. I think it was 6 in the morning when I made it home.

My wife fussed and argued, saying that I was no good. I made up a lie and said the car stopped on me. I said the tire was flat and I was out of town. The lady told me that if I came back she would cook me steaks. "Show nuff!" I put on my clothes at 6 p.m. and got in my car and went back to her house. She had two girls and was so nice to me--nicer than my wife would ever be. I stayed with her until 3 a.m. the next morning.

I went home so drunk and high that I really didn't know how to get in the door. My wife got up and pulled me in and started beating on me. She said that if I was going to keep doing this to get out and leave. I told her I wasn't going anywhere because I had bought the house and the land. If anybody goes, she would go.

I must have passed out on the couch. I woke up at about 6 am that Sunday morning. I took my pistol and put it under the couch. She came back with her father. He was a deacon in the church and she was the secretary. Putting a rifle to my face he said, "I will kill you if you hurt my daughter." A bad, evil spirit said, "You can kill him in your own house and you can get off." I didn't and said no to that spirit. I told it to just leave me alone.

My wife asked me to leave. Turning 25 years old that day, I made it back to my friend's house—the one I had been with all night. I didn't have any of my clothes. I was able to go to work that Monday—working across the field. Not seeing my wife, I made up my mind to not go back. Working in the field, I was back and forth between my mom's new house and my friend's.

My dad told me, "One day son, you need to go back home and get a divorce, because people are talking about you." I told my dad that it was going to work out. I believe that there is a power that watches over me. So, here I am in a place where I am being loved and cared for. At home, it wasn't that way. My wife was always complaining, arguing, and cutting me down.

I said to myself, "I married her and I'm going to try and make it work." And before that day was over I went to my friend's house who had just come from the doctor. She was pregnant. I was married and had gotten a woman pregnant. After a month, I went to my wife's house and told her that I wanted to come back home. I believed we could make it. There was one condition: if she would accept the child that my friend was going to have.

She said "no" and started crying and saying that she could not accept someone else's baby. She said to go and leave her alone. I asked her to forgive me before I left and she said refused. I went back to my friend's house that night and it seemed like she had everything going her way.

I was still praying. My mother said one evening that a woman had called from Albany. The lady said to be in a particular place if I wanted a job. I didn't know who it was, but I went to work that morning out across the field. The owner I was working for came to me and said Miller Brewers wanted to hire me and he told them I already had a job.

I went back to work—sad. I strolled away from the other guys to pray and ask the Lord for help and directions. At the age of 25, I was made a peanut sampler. My boss said I was very intelligent and gave me a $1.00 raise to keep me. About eight months later, I drove to Tifton, Georgia in his Cadillac. I stopped in Albany on my way back to the unemployment office.

I was sent to W, G & L. I didn't know anything about Albany. I had an interview with one of the directors who asked me if I knew anything about meters or reading them. I told him more about the meters than he knew because I had worked with meters in Florida. He said he would hire me but I lived in Randolph County, which was at least 35 miles away. I told him that all I needed was a chance.

He said he was going to hire me and told me to be at work that following Monday morning. I left praising God. I went back to Shellman in my boss' car. I didn't tell him whether I would be back at work or not.

When the weekend came, I got dress and went to be with my friend who was going to have the baby. I partied all that weekend. One of my brothers came home. Riding on the dark road, there was a cow in the middle of the road. I hit the cow and totaled my car. When the police arrived the cow was back out across the field.

There was a voice telling me, "I'm going to kill you." I was high on marijuana. The Lord had saved me again.

I went to work in Albany—leaving and returning to Shellman when it was dark. It was work out reading meters and they started me off with $3.18 an hour. It was very exciting and I wanted to learn it.

In every box that was opened up, there was a black widow spider or a snake. It was a dangerous job. I was taught to be careful. Six months later I was offered another position as a Service Technician that paid $9.00 an hour. Look at God work! I shouted and went to buy some drugs to have a good time.

My son was born. I moved him, his mother and her two daughters to Albany. In 1982, $9.00 an hour was pretty good money. So, here I go again—making money and living a fast life. I enjoyed my job. I was modeling at a club in Albany. I would go to Florida and buy lottery tickets and come back to the club and throw them in the air for people to catch.

I was being blessed in spite of my wrongs, hatred, and refusal to serve the Lord.

8

SETBACK FOR MAJOR COMEBACK

My girlfriends had died. He had told us before that we better get there on a plane or come fast. The town was fifty miles away. We just laughed. We knew that he had money. He was a retired veteran that was wounded in Vietnam. When we made it to the house, we looked and could not find anything.

By him being in a wheelchair I pick up the pillow out of the chair. I turned the pillow over and it was packed with $20,000.00. I told my fiancé we should look in the other car. There we found another pillow with $20,000.00. I didn't want to take the whole $40,000.00 because I respected my fiancé. We left one pillow so her father could find it and we took $20,000.00 for ourselves.

I was wild and partying, and I didn't know how to handle money. I believe today that the Lord left that for me. I was raising my hands in the air like I just didn't care. Everyone was hollering, "cowboy, cowboy." I was the life of the party.

All of my coworkers wanted to be around me because there was joy and happiness. I didn't know it was a gift that God had given me. While working at W, G & Light Commission in 1968, I discovered a 3 and 6-year-old left alone in a house. The temperature had climbed to a life-threatening 105 degrees.

I was a Service Technician for 10 years and immediately notified the police from my radio-equipped truck. I stayed with the children until the proper authorities could take over. I was promoted to the title of Power Pac the official mascot of the Operation Kids program. An Operation Kids article was featured in Public Power magazine in the May - June 1990 edition.

On June 14, 1990, I received a letter from George Bush extending congratulations on my participation in the American Public Power Association Community Service Awards Ceremony.

Although I loved my job and enjoyed the atmosphere, I could still see the racism on the job. My supervisor hated that I was being recognized. I could still feel something missing in my life. My girlfriend and I seem like we were drinking more. The love wasn't there anymore. We started arguing and fighting.

I know that it was the Lord that brought us out of the cotton field.

In 1992, I had not been to a church for over 30 years. I heard a voice on a Friday night after drinking two fifths of Courvoisier Cognac say, "You're going to die." I looked around and said, "Who said that?" In my sin, I could feel the presence of a Supreme Being.

I cried out, "Lord, forgive me." I was sick and felt bad all that Saturday. My friend showed me that she didn't care by leaving me home all day. She went to her girlfriend's house. I prayed while I was alone like never before. I just wanted a chance. That Sunday I wanted to go to church.

We went to church. We heard the preacher say the streets in heaven were paved with gold, and these arms were undeveloped wings and that we would be able to fly all over heaven. My flesh said, "Ugh ugh! I'll get saved and go to heaven and steal some gold and fly out of heaven." I could come back and open up another night club. By that time, I can't explain it, but the Spirit of the living God hit me. I started shouting, jumping and praising God. I felt good and asked for forgiveness in my praising. I fell on the floor asking the Lord to come into my heart and to forgive me for all my sins. A change came over me. What a change!

I joined church Sunday and that evening at 6 pm, my fiancé was putting on some clothes. I asked her where she was going. She was going to the Legion. I said, "We are saved now." She said that I was saved—not her. It seemed like a dark cloud came over me and my heart melted. I still loved her and we stayed together.

Now praying about it, I went back to church the next Sunday. I asked the preacher to marry us right after service. We got married, and that same evening she went to the Legion. I knew it wasn't right, but I started praying more.

The Lord spoke to me and instructed me to go

through. This is how my people turned their back on me. The word said, "Don't turn around and don't look back. I got you in my hands."

Can you image the heartache that I was going through? I believe that the Lord was showing me that after all I had done in my life, my heart was now being broken. I wanted more of the Lord and His word. This is the only way we can make it with the Lord.

As long as we were in the world together, the first eight years were great. At that point I was praying and being humble and asking the Lord to use me. After six months of being in church, my pastor came and asked me if I would consider being a deacon. He said that I had not missed Sunday school or bible study in six months. He had chosen two other men to be deacons, but they hardly came. He considered me to be faithful. I accepted.

Teaching bible study and Sunday school made me a better man. I could see that things were changing in my life. I was growing in the Lord even though I was dealing with marital problems. The Lord told me to go to Shellman every other Saturday to see my mother because she was sick. Some people said she had cancer, but the doctor said he could not find anything.

When we started talking she said, "Baby, take me to see a root worker." I told her no. The enemy had made her mind to believe in the root workers or two-headed people. I started praying and praying for my mom to get the curse off of her. I started teaching her about Jesus. The older preachers didn't talk about Jesus. All they talked about was God. But God so loved the world that He sent His only begotten son, and whosoever believed in him shall not perish but shall have everlasting life.

My mom always wanted me to tell her about Jesus. I would also sing gospel songs to her. She confessed Jesus Christ as her Lord and Savior. My mother was dedicated in the Baptist church. She started going to a Holiness church. Then her mind seemed to be clear that it was all about Jesus. She told me that she was glad to be saved and that I taught her about Jesus. She believed that was my reason for returning home.

As a deacon, I had to stand face to face with the devil. The chairman called me one night and said his heart was hurting because he caught the pastor of the church with a young girl. I told him to pray and try not to worry about it. He told me that he loved the church.

That Sunday morning, I got a call around 6 a.m. saying that the chairman of the deacon board, who was my friend, had died of a heart attack. I had just recently spoken with him. I was the only one that he called before he died. My heart was broken again. Being a Christian, I knew that I had to be strong. No one confronted the pastor.

Out of twelve deacons, I was the only one that had been there for about eight months. The rest had been there for most of their lives. The pastor called me into his office and asked me if I would accept the chairman of the deacons' board position. He said there were eleven more deacons and that I was the only one saved. I accepted the position and I prayed and fasted.

The Lord showed me that I was going to be sat up and he could use me. It went on with the preacher doing wrong. The members and the other deacons were looking at me. We approached the pastor in the office about the matter. Again he said that none of the deacons was saved except for me. He pulled out his gun and told us to get out of his office. He didn't want to talk to any of us.

I asked them what they were doing and one of deacons said that salt makes evil spirits run. I said that I didn't believe in that because it's witchcraft and is for root workers. Another deacon said we should go see a man he knew in Alabama that got his son out of prison. I told them that we had to get that out of our minds. I said, "This is God's house." I finally convinced them that the Lord would take care of all of us.

The next week, the loan company that we financed the church through called me and another member that was on the finance committee. Three thousand dollars was needed by 5 p.m. that evening or they would put the lock on the door at the church. We came up with $15,000.00 each.

Two days later, I was called back to Shellman. My mom had fallen and was sick. We rushed her to the hospital. She cried and told us that she was sick. Two of my sisters and I were at her bedside. I asked her if she remembered what I told her. She said, "Yeah baby. You taught me about the Lord Jesus." She said that she confessed Him and doesn't have to hurt anymore.

My mother said she had seen her sister who had passed six months earlier in a dream. She said her sister told her to come to where she was. We headed home to Albany and left her in the hospital and my baby sister stayed with her.

9

ACCEPTING JESUS CHRIST AS LORD

By the time we arrived back to Albany my mother had passed. It really hurts when you know a person has left this world and have gone to the other side. I know my mom was better off being with the Lord. There was no more pain, sorrow, or tears. The next weekend we set up her funeral. Members of my family were drinking alcohol as we tried to put together the obituary. I told them to respect my mother during this time. Some of the family got mad. I told them to go home. I loved my mother and wanted to remember her as happy, joyous and lovely. I knew she had accepted Jesus and that she was in heaven.

I didn't preach my mother's funeral. I was a deacon at that time. Thank God that he brought me through all the pain and sorrow.

Back at the church, we were still dealing with trouble. I wanted to speak out and tell the people what was happening. I was confronted by a deacon who told me I better not say anything about it. If I did, I was going to die.

One Sunday I stood up and told the preacher that I wanted to talk to the church. He told me to sit down. I prayed right there and asked the Lord if I should just leave it alone. The Spirit of the Lord strengthened me. I couldn't sit down anymore. I told him that he had babies in the church. The Lord told me to tell the church since he had threatened all the deacons.

And he said out of his mouth, "Who gave you the right to tell the church?" I told him that God gave me the right. The preacher said, "I'm taking you down. You are no longer a deacon of the church, so get out!" By that time the rest of the deacons and all the members stood up and said, "Deacon Fairbanks, don't you go anywhere." They told the preacher that he needed to leave. He finally left. Some of the members came running to me and thanked me for saving the church. I told them that I didn't do it, but God did it.

Some of them said they had seen fire coming out of my mouth when I told the preacher that God did it. Some were angry with me because some of their grandchildren were in the church. I want to live holy and not judge anybody, but when the Lord gives you something to do, you better do it.

When you think the devil is gone, he is still around. The next Saturday we came together for a meeting at the church. When we got there the deacons ran up to me and said the preacher still had the keys and that there will be no voting at the church. He had five more preachers inside the church. Right then, I told the people to pray. There were about 100 people outside the church who wanted to vote him out.

After praying, we went into the church and confronted that spirit. The police officer who was with him said that he didn't want any deacons in the church. The police officer was there to enforce that. The other preachers tried to talk to me and bribe me. If I let him stay there, they would make me a preacher. All I had to do was say so. If you are reading this book, you can't compromise with the devil! I told them "no." About that time the police made us get out of the church.

I said, "Lord what do you want me to do?" I went to the telephone next door to the church. The word of the Lord came to me as plain as day to call the police department. I called to speak to the commanding officer. I told him that an officer was in the church and would not let the members inside. We stood on the outside. When he came, the officer was confronted and asked what they were doing there. And they said that there had been a funeral earlier and they helped with the procession.

I spoke and said we didn't have a funeral and they were blocking us from coming into the church by the pastor's demands. The commanding police said he couldn't put state and church together. We went inside to have the meeting. The preacher came out of the office and said it was an unlawful meeting. He told me that I would never be anything. By that time, another preacher told him we had voted him out and that he should leave. Everyone started praising the Lord.

We went nine months without a preacher. The members wanted to pay off some bills and expenses of the church and wanted to wait to get another pastor. I told them they needed a pastor.

The devil came to me and said, "Nobody is saved at this church. Just take the money and leave." I remember that was what the preacher said—that no one was saved. We finally called a preacher. Some of the members were mad, but I thought he was the best man for the job. He accepted the job.

After a month of being pastor, he told the people that if they didn't come to bible school that they couldn't sing in the choir. I went to him and said, "Let them get to know you." He said, "no." It went across my mind that Satan was over the choir in heaven. And sure enough, some of the choir members pushed some of the deacons up to throw him out the door. I went running to see what was going on. One of the men came up to me with his eyes crooked—like they were in the back of his head. The deacon said, "You want some of this too"? I pulled off my coat and a voice came to me and said not to do it.

I left the church and twelve members started having church at my house. I remembered I was still over the finances at the other church. So I went and got a cashier's check for $10,000.00 and turned it back over to the deacon. We had about thirty members and found a building. We had been fellowshipping for about six months and had voted on a name. The same preacher that was put out of the church and who also left with us told us that he didn't want "Baptist" on the church sign. I said that denomination didn't mean anything as long as we were serving Jesus. He told us that he was the pastor and the founder and there would be no voting on the name. My heart just melted right there.

I told him I could not be under any leadership like that. We had voted on it and he said "no." I left that night and never went back. Wandering from church to church, I fasted and prayed. Finally, my wife left and joined another church and some people went back to the original church.

Fasting and praying, I asked the Lord what he wanted me to do. After 4 months, my wife wanted me to join her church. We were going through some things and she wanted her pastor to counsel her. I accepted counseling. When we meet, he told me I needed to come and be with my family.

I couldn't be with my family because I had told the pastor that my wife had an affair. The pastor asked me to forgive her and I told him I couldn't forgive her because she had more than one affair. The pastor asked how many affairs she'd had. She admitted to two. My life was messed up.

I heard a voice say, "Go back to the church—the first church you joined." On a Wednesday night, I told the members I was coming back, and they welcomed me back. We were having bible study in the cold with no heat. Both heaters were out in the church. After bible study the deacons opened up to me about a young man who had swindled them out of ten thousand dollars. They didn't have the money to replace the heaters. The next day I paid three thousand dollars to have a heater put in. A few people were happy because I was back, and a few weren't. They didn't want me over any auxiliaries because I had left. I prayed and asked the Lord why he sent me back. I know the Lord speaks because He showed me in a dream how I was going to be blessed.

Six months after being back, the church didn't have a preacher. I told them they needed to call a preacher. After a preacher was called to the church, I was made a Sunday school and bible study teacher. I said, "Lord, you doing this for me?" Trouble was still in the home.

My wife said out of her mouth that she didn't want to be married to a preacher. I told her I was a deacon, not a preacher. That Sunday as I went to church, I told my pastor that I needed to talk to him. He said he knew what I wanted to talk about. He said he knew that God had called me to minister. I told him that's what I wanted to talk to him about. I kept hearing these voices telling me to minister the gospel. He said the Lord had showed him in a dream.

My wife divorced me and walked out. I asked, "How can I minister Gods word?" My wife took everything from me, including my home. When I met her she didn't have anything. So I went to my pastor and asked him what I should do. He told me that he was going to license and ordain me as a minister. He told me that God was working with me. The enemy will always try to stop your destiny.

In the divorce, I could have gotten her for adultery, but the Spirit said not to. The enemy thought he had me. During court, there was a chance that I would pay alimony, child support, equity from the house and $5,000 in legal fees. Don't tell me God don't work! The judge asked me what I thought my wife deserved. I told the judge she had a job, our son was twelve years old, and she moved out of the house before the divorce settled.

The judge ruled that she doesn't deserve anything else and to let her go with what she had gotten out of the house. The devil stood up in the court room—her and the attorney. The lawyer asked the judge why I couldn't pay child support and the attorney fee. The judge said, "I'm the judge. No legal fees, child support or attorney fees."

I jumped up in the air and praised my God. My ex-wife had the nerve to say that I thought I was something. I said, "My God is awesome!"

10

PUTTING THE PAST BEHIND

After all of that I was free to get closer to the Lord. I prayed, cried and thanked the Lord and out of the blue a preacher called me. He said that he saw me in a dream. He said that a church needed a preacher for Easter Sunday. He asked me if I would be able to go. I told him I needed to check with my pastor and I would call him back. My pastor said it was fine and I called him back. He told me the members of this particular church were disappointed because they had asked one of the bishops' son to come, but two days before the service, he called and said that he could not make it.

I went that Sunday to preach and we fell in love with one another. They asked me to come back to start bible study that Wednesday. I agreed. Before I went there that night, the Lord had blessed me with a new car. When I pulled up at the church, I could see the people praising God and dancing in the church. When I got out of the car, I said, "You all are praising God!" They said with a laugh, "Minister Fairbanks, you are our Pastor." I asked, "how do you all know?" One of the members had dreamed that the pastor would come on a Wednesday night in a white car with cowboy boots on.

I fit the description and we all started praising the Lord. They said they didn't call a pastor unless he had a wife, but the Lord had showed me to them, and they wanted to obey the Lord. Everyone at the church started being blessed with cars, houses and material things.

An addition was added onto the church building. I was still lonely and praying to the Lord for a companion. There was a lot of temptation being the pastor of the church. Everybody was trying to give me somebody. I know I could have moved, but I wanted to wait on the Lord.

After three years of being a Pastor, I met this friend. She told me that she had changed and was a licensed Evangelist. We got together and went to a movie. I know people do change. We started dating. About two months later, she called me and said she was going home after church. I told her that I would see her the next day.

The Lord will never lead you wrong. That Monday I went by the shop where she worked. She wasn't at the shop and the young man that was riding in my work truck went by her house. I thought she may have been sick. When I knocked on the door, a young man came to the door and I asked for her. He said, "Oh, you're the preacher." He said that they had gotten back together again. He told me to leave and I did. Twenty minutes later she called me saying that she was very sorry and that the devil made her do it.

I had to visit her father, who was a pastor and tell him what happened. It really hurt because I thought she was the one that the Lord had sent me. Three days went by and the door bell rang at 1 a.m. When I came to the door, I asked who it was and she told me. I unlocked the door and asked her what she wanted. She started crying and I let her in the door.

She told me her father said that if I didn't marry her, the other guy would. I told her that I wasn't going to marry her and to go ahead and marry him. She said I had to marry her so she could keep her license to minister. By that time, she pushed me over on the back of the couch. She hollered, "Stop, please stop!" and she raped me. I had been celibate for three years. She asked me, "Now are you going to marry me?" I told her "no" and asked her to leave.

My heart was broken. After she left I jumped in the shower with tears in my eyes. I cleaned myself and got out of the shower. I prayed the rest of the morning, asking the Lord God to forgive me for my sins. I know I was forgiven because the Holy Spirit had told me that I didn't want it, and I was forced.

God knows who loves him and who is trying to obey him. That's why He said His eyes are upon the righteous, His ears open to the righteous cry and His face is against those who do evil. I went on to church that Sunday. The members always tried to give me somebody. I could not tell them that I had been raped. They probably would have laughed at me. Prayer changes things.

A new lady had started working with me on my job. One day I was talking with her and asked her if she had any friends that I could talk to. She told me that she didn't have any friends from Albany because she was new here. She told me she had a sister. I asked her, "Is she pretty like you?" I wanted to meet her. She told me her sister lived in Lexington, Kentucky. I said, "That's almost eight hundred miles from Albany!" She said her sister was supposed to be in Albany in July. I wanted a chance to meet her.

I was still pastoring and ministering the gospel. I went from one Sunday to three Sundays a month. That was a battle against the enemy, but I stood my ground. In other words, I stood on the Lord's word. Months had gone by and July had gone by. My friend who told me about her sister moved on to work at a bank. When God has something for you, keep holding on. I am a living witness. I went to the bank and I was surprised to see her. She said her sister did not come to visit and she wanted to give me her telephone number.

I waited about two weeks before I called her. I figured they had talked and I didn't want her sister to think I was easy. I finally called her and the first thing she wanted to know was if there was something wrong with her. I said, "No, but God said a man that finds a wife, finds a good thing." It was God that was leading me. After two weeks of talking on the telephone, we became friends.

The Lord led me to Kentucky. I had never been that way before. I made it to Lexington and got settled in. She said she would pick me up around 6 p.m. after work so we could go out to dinner. When we laid eyes on each other, the Lord said, "That's the one." We went out to dinner that Friday. That Saturday morning, she came to pick me up so I could meet her mom and dad. I knew that we didn't have anything in common but the Lord.

My prayer was, "Lord, give me a wife who loves you as much as I love you. And I know we'll be able to make it." That Sunday morning, she said she would come to get me for church. When we got to the church, it was very large. I could count about fifty men and about five hundred women. I said to myself, "Lord, did you do this for me?" It seemed like God just opened up heaven and poured me out a blessing. They took me into the pastor's office. We talked and he said, "I know you didn't come eight hundred miles to see me." I said, "No, I came to visit one of your members." We had service, and after service was over, a lot of ladies gathered around me saying, "You are a pastor from Albany, Georgia." And they asked who I came to see. I told them I was on a mission from the Lord to get me a wife.

I left Lexington that Sunday with joy in my heart. I praised God for eight hundred miles back home. I got home and called some of my family members. They asked me if I was going crazy. They asked if there were no women in Georgia and all kinds of questions. They said I am a pastor and didn't know anything about her. I knew she was a God-fearing woman.

In about three months, I asked her to come to Georgia and visit us at the church. She agreed to come. I picked her up from the airport in Atlanta that Saturday. I took her to church to meet some of the members. We were having a Christmas celebration. Some of the members got angry because I wouldn't have anything to do with who they wanted me to have. I learned that what is for me is for me.

Growing stronger in my situations of life, a couple of months later I drove back to Lexington. I had a preaching engagement. Long distance relationships do not last. How many of you all know that? I wanted to ask her to marry me then, but the Lord said to wait.

Still without a companion, people tried to take me down. I was praying, fasting and letting the Lord lead me. He asked me to invite her to come down to Georgia for a holiday. I went to pick her up at the airport. While driving, my speed got up to eighty miles an hour. I was getting ready to pop the question. She asked me why I was driving so fast. I told her to open the glove compartment and give me the white box. I said, "I know that we haven't known each other for four or five months, but will you marry me?" She opened up the box with the one carat ring inside. And I said it again. "Will you marry me?" A smile came over her face, and she said that if I slowed my driving, she would.

She asked when we were going to get married. I told her the following month, and she agreed. She put her house up for sale and it was sold within a month. It was at that time that her two children were getting out of school for the summer. We knew God was working because everything was falling into place.

She moved to Albany, Georgia. At that point the pastor had a wife that the Lord had given him. Everybody was so happy. The members of the church gave us a reception. Most of her family members came from all over.

After we were married for about three months, the enemy attacked us one night at midnight. I received a call that my son had been shot. Then it was expressed that he wasn't going to live too much longer and we needed to come to the hospital. I prayed before I left the house. When we arrived at the hospital, they said they weren't sure if my son was going to make it. I said, "He's going to make it because God assured me that it wasn't his time yet."

A nurse came out and said that he was gone, but that he's breathing again. I know that God answers prayers. So time went on and he got better.

11

THE SPIRITUAL MAN

The Lord is still ordering my steps. Pastoring the church had gotten harder. Some of the members said that I was a hired servant and they didn't really want a pastor, but through it all, my wife and I stayed for six and a half years. We finally left.

We were riding a week later and I told my wife I know that God has something for me to do. We saw a building for sale. I went up to the building and looked around. I laid my hands on the outside of the building. In His own way, the Lord showed me that was where He wanted us—New Vision Ministries.

Another blessing showed me how God works. The following Wednesday I called the lady that owned the building. She told me what they wanted for it. She said that black people don't buy commercial property. I said that I wanted to buy this property. She would have to get back to me after everything was checked out with my credit and everything.

I looked around and saw all the prostitutes and the drug people walking the streets. I prayed right there, thanking the Lord for letting me be on this street. She said, "Mr. Fairbanks, you really want it—don't you?" I said, "Yes, I do." She asked me if I had a down payment. I told her I could put five hundred dollars down and that was all I had. I told her my credit was messed up, but I knew God was going to fix it.

I know that prayer changes things. Friday of that week she called me and asked when we could close. I told her that evening would work, and we closed on the building. If you're reading this book, the Lord did it. We started New Vision Ministries with seven people and we've been blessed tremendously through the power of God.

We went out into the neighborhood and gave out flyers and invited everyone to come to church. Friends of mine said, "You're on Highland Avenue where all the prostitutes are! Why don't you move somewhere else?" This is where God wanted us to be. Most churches were moving out of the city, but my heart was right there on Highland Avenue. I know the Lord has already worked it out.

Going to church on Sunday mornings, I would see prostitutes and drug addicts sitting next door to the church. It really hurt me. We called the police and they said they couldn't do anything about it because we didn't own the building. I prayed and asked the Lord what to do about the prostitutes and the building next door. And the Lord said to buy it. We didn't have any money. Saints, it doesn't always take money.

I called the lady that owned the building and asked the selling price and if she would sell it to the church. It was a rundown building, and she was asking thirty thousand dollars. I didn't know where I was going to get the money. The Lord showed me that I had it in my 401K. I took ten thousand dollars out and made a down payment and financed the rest.

We were able to buy the building and remodel. I know that God placed us here for a good reason. We can help people in the community. The newspaper wrote an article about us being in the neighborhood in March 2008. I also received my Drug & Alcohol Counseling Diploma. The Lord will keep working in your life for better things.

In 2010, I received my Doctrine in Divinity from the Rainbow School of Ministry and all sorts of awards. I just wanted to do more for the Lord. I have seen people come and go in the ministry—having a mind religion but not a heart religion. Everyday I pray the Lord would elevate me higher and that my life or the words I say about Jesus will help somebody.

I thank God for my wife who is always there for me. New Vision Ministries Church is growing strong. The Lord showed me how a man can be changed from walking in flesh to walking in the spirit.

I haven't given up yet and the Lord has not given up on me. The Lord keeps taking me higher in His word. Now I am able to see the attacks of the enemy and the way he works. Through God's grace and mercy, I tell everybody that we can't fight the enemy, which is Satan himself. You have to seek God with your whole heart and not just sometimes. He will make a way.

I give glory to God, His son Jesus, who is my Savior, and of the world, and the Holy Spirit. The Holy Spirit comforts me when I don't know what to do. Let this book be for the Father, the Son, and the Holy Ghost. Whoever reads it, may God open their eyes to see the blessings He has already prepared for mankind. Amen.

ABOUT THE AUTHOR

Dr. Kenneth Fairbanks is a native of Shellman, Georgia, and was born February 21, 1954. He is son of the late Willie B. and Maggie Lee Fairbanks. He is married to Mrs. Nerita Higgins Fairbanks from Lexington, Kentucky. They are the parents of Tammy, Tonya, Kenneth Jr., Patrick, Robert and Jason.

Dr. Kenneth Fairbanks professed Jesus Christ in 1990, under the leadership of Reverend Homer Davis at New Testament Baptist Church. He was called by God to preach the gospel in 1997 and was licensed to minister by Reverend William Spears. Later in 2000, he was ordained and received a Doctor of Divinity Degree in 2010 from the Rainbow School of Seminary Ministry in Alachua, Florida by Dr. E.B. Tate, Ph.D.

Dr. Kenneth Fairbanks serves as Pastor of New Vision Ministries in Albany, Georgia that was founded in October 2005. He has directed the church's spiritual and numerical growth. His motto at New Vision Ministries is "PUSH PUSH PUSH—Pray Until Something Happens."

Made in the USA
Columbia, SC
01 August 2022

64428483R00045